Herdsmen and their animals at rest on a hillside, from a nineteenth-century oil painting.

The Drovers

Shirley Toulson

Published by Shire Publications Ltd,
Midland House, West Way, Botley, Oxford OX2 0PH.
(www.shirebooks.co.uk)

British Library Cataloguing in Publication Data:
Toulson, Shirley
The drovers. – 2nd ed. – (Shire album; 45)
1. Drovers – Great Britain – History
2. Cattle trails – Great Britain – History
I. Title 636'.083
ISBN-10: 0 7478 0630 6.
ISBN-13: 978 0 74780 630 1

Cover: *A Smithfield drover, from W. H. Pyne's 'The Costume of Great Britain' (1805). His drover's licence can clearly be seen fastened to his left arm.*

ACKNOWLEDGEMENTS
Photographs and other illustrations are acknowledged as follows: Beamish, North of England Open Air Museum, page 55 (top); Mervyn Benford, page 25 (bottom right); Malcolm Boyes, page 11 (top); Thomas Fall, page 28; Cadbury Lamb, pages 3, 9 (top), 11 (bottom), 13 (bottom), 16, 21 (bottom), 22, 23 (bottom), 25 (bottom left), 34 (bottom), 36, 37 (bottom), 38, 40, 45 (bottom), 46, 50, 51 (bottom), 54, 55 (bottom); Lloyd's Bank Archives, page 9 (bottom); Jane Miller, page 17; National Museum of Wales, Welsh Folk Museum, page 4; Jim Proudfoot, page 32-3; Sue Ross, pages 5, 45 (top) and 52; Lien Seinen, page 29; Graham Swanson, page 19; Shirley Toulson, pages 10, 34 (top), 45 (centre), 48, 49 (both), 51 (top); West Suffolk Record Office, page 18; Gwyneth Wilson, pages 14, 21 (top); Wycombe Chair and Local History Museum, page 25 (top); Diana Zeuner, page 23 (top). The maps are by Richard G. Holmes. National Grid references are used with the permission of the Controller of Her Majesty's Stationary Office.

Printed by PrintOnDemand-Worldwide.com, Peterborough, UK.

Contents

In June 2004 the road into Smithfield Market in London was turfed over to recreate a drove for the Architectural Biennial Celebration.

Sylvanus Evans was a drover from Llan Ffestiniog, Gwynedd, Wales.

Introduction

In 2003 the great cattle market at Banbury in Oxfordshire closed down. It was one of the last such markets in England and its loss emphasises the brutalising change that has come over the industry now that cattle and sheep are taken many miles in lorries to central abattoirs or even shipped live to the Continent. These long journeys are made over major roads that bear little resemblance to the highways walked by the drovers, who spent three weeks or more bringing cattle from Wales to Smithfield in London or from Scotland to East Anglia.

From the departure of the Romans to the making of the toll roads in the eighteenth century no main public highways were built in Britain. People paved some paths as local need arose or travelled the old trade routes, many of which were ridgeway paths dating from prehistoric times and still used today by walkers. These paths were used by lines of heavily burdened packhorses carrying essential goods, of which salt was the most important. They also took wool from the farms and lead, tin and even coal from the mines and quarries.

For centuries, from the time of the Norman Conquest (and probably before that) to the establishment of the railways, the drovers were the main users of these old routes. They were bringing the black cattle from Wales and the Scottish Highlands to English pastures for fattening before they were sold in the markets of the south-east, the best price of all being realised at Smithfield market.

Droves of livestock formed great cavalcades that blocked the way for other travellers for hours at a time; and they were as noisy as they were spectacular, with the chief drovers riding alongside the beasts, the cattle dogs barking and the men shouting out one of the oldest and most universal of human cries, rendered in Welsh as *heiptrw hw* and transcribed by Sir Walter Scott as *hoo-hoo*. This sound is still used wherever men drive cattle, and the drovers used it to warn farmers along their routes that they were coming, as well as to urge on their own loitering beasts. It was important that such a warning be given, and in good time, for if farmers did not want their cattle instinctively to join the drove they had to make sure they were safely enclosed.

Some parts of the droveways were also used to transport pigs, sheep, geese and turkeys, and these creatures too had to travel great distances. Sheep from the Wiltshire Downs were taken along the Oxfordshire and Berkshire Ridgeway and then the Icknield Way across the Chilterns and Suffolk to Thetford market in Norfolk; and going in the opposite direction were flocks of East Anglian turkeys driven south-westward to Smithfield, roosting each night in the trees by the wayside. But it was the cattle drovers who were the aristocrats of their trade, and this book concentrates on them.

The drovers

For centuries the economic survival of Scotland and Wales depended upon the price the drovers were able to get for the mountain cattle. So it was the roast beef of old England that kept the drovers in business, although they and the farmers, who originally owned the cattle, hardly ever knew such rich eating. Their staple diet was oats and the only flesh they ate, and that very rarely, was pork, mutton and salt herring. Sir Walter Scott, who must have had it on the authority of his drover grandfather, tells readers of his short story *The Two Drovers* that for his long journey south the Highland drover relied on 'a few handfuls of oatmeal, and two or three onions, renewed from time to time, and a ram's horn filled with whisky, which he used regularly, but sparingly, every night and morning'.

Despite this meagre fare, the drovers were among the most respected people in the farming communities of their homelands. In the eighteenth and early nineteenth centuries a Welsh drover could earn as much as 3 shillings a day, while his contemporary working on the farms would do well to earn as much as 1s 6d a day in the summer months, when he was expected to labour from 5 a.m. to 8.30 p.m. As well as being

This wayside encounter between a drover and a village girl is from a set of drawings by Thomas Sidney Cooper, published in 1839.

comparatively rich, the drovers who were entrusted with so much of their countrymen's wealth had to he honest and reliable despite their wandering life.

From Tudor times, to ensure the enforcement of the vagrancy laws, each drover had to be licensed. To qualify for a licence he had to prove that he was over thirty, a householder and a married man. At that time a license cost 12d at Quarter Sessions plus a further 8d for registering it with a clerk of the peace. By 1671, Scottish drovers as well as Welsh had to carry a certificate of respectability. With all such safeguards, drovers were considered to be so trustworthy that in the reign of Charles I they were made responsible for carrying the Ship Money from Wales to London, an example that inspired Cromwell to use them as tax collectors.

So although there are wild tales of semi-legendary drovers such as the famous Highlander Rob Roy, for the most part they were solid worthies, trusted by their neighbours to ensure the economic survival of the community, carry money and important documents as well as cattle to the south and bring home goods and news of the outside world to the remote farmsteads. They were the reporters of the time, who were the first to hear and tell of the outcome of the Battle of Waterloo, and to whom the farmers' wives turned for information about the latest fashions.

Above all they were responsible for the large sums of money which the cattle represented, on the hoof on the outward journey and homeward in hard cash. This wealth had to be taken through remote mountain passes haunted by highwaymen and brigands of every sort. Nor was it unknown for human greed to get the better of less successful drovers, and there are a few sad stories of fratricide along the green lanes. The obvious solution was to devise a safe means of transferring cash without having to carry it about. So the history of banking is closely linked to droving and particularly to the career of David Jones, who first came into contact with the drovers outside the family farm, when he was employed at the age of fifteen at the King's Head in Llandovery, Carmarthenshire, where they conducted much of their business. This led him to found his Bank of the Black Ox in Llandovery in 1799. John Jones, grandson of David Jones, ran the Llandeilo branch after his grandfather died in 1839. The bank was then known as Jones's Bank and cheques were issued with the imprint of the Black Ox until Lloyds took it over early in the First World War.

Generally, a drove would be made up of some four or five hundred head of cattle, divided into manageable herds with three or four drovers and their dogs in charge of each one. Many of them could expect to be on the road for the best part of a month; the journey from North Wales to the Kent pastures certainly could not be done in under three weeks. Although the droves were not immune from attack, accompanying them did provide some security, so frequently other travellers would join the cavalcade.

By the nineteenth century the more prosperous Welsh drovers were mounted and sold their horses along with the cattle in the English markets and made the return journey by coach. They also looked after themselves well on the eastward journey with the cattle. For they worked out their routes and timing in order to have overnight accommodation at inns, where their coming was often the occasion for great festivity, with wrestling and boxing matches arranged between the farmers and the drovers. The Highlanders, according to Sir Walter Scott, lived more sparsely, sleeping out of doors with the cattle, and many of them not once resting under a roof 'during a journey on foot from Lochaber to Lincolnshire'.

The King's Head Inn at Llandovery (above) where David Jones founded his Bank of the Black Ox and (below) one of the banknotes issued by the Llandeilo branch.

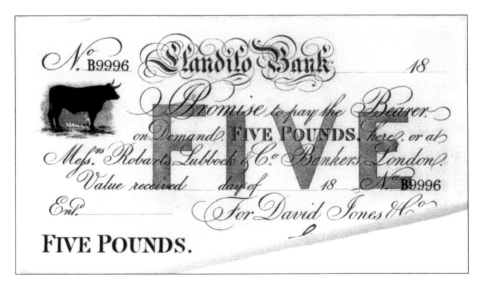

For both Scots and Welsh drovers the first consideration was always the grazing of the beasts, as was shown by a Welsh-speaking inn owner at Stockbridge in Hampshire, who promised *Gwair tymherus porfa flasas* (worthwhile grass and a pleasant pasture) before going on to mention *Cwrw da cwal cysurus* (good beer and a comfortable shelter). You can still see his inscription, kept freshly painted on the old inn, now a private house, to the west of the town.

That is a rare survival. Yet although in many cases all traces of the old drovers' inns have completely disappeared, you can still track down their whereabouts by patches of bright grass, owing its lushness to centuries of manuring by the visiting herds. Halfpenny pastures they are often called, reflecting the cost of grazing per night per beast, and the name lingers on in the names of many fields and adjoining lanes. The standard charge for a night's accommodation for a drover, for the last two hundred years of the droving era, fluctuated between 4d and 6d.

Over the centuries their dress varied little, although Scots and Welsh prepared themselves rather differently for their long journeys. Sir Walter Scott's Robin Oig wore the Highland bonnet, the plaid, in which he concealed his dirk, the kilt and tartan hose gartered beneath his knees. He must have looked like the Highland drover in Landseer's painting in the Victoria and Albert Museum, bidding goodbye to his new baby, his weeping wife and his aged father before departing for the south. Other paintings of drovers in the north of England show them wearing trews or trousers, but these may represent Lowlanders or even Yorkshiremen.

A former drovers' inn at Stockbridge in Hampshire with its welcome in Welsh.

The ruins of Limekiln House, an old drovers' inn which stood on the heights of the Hambleton Drove in North Yorkshire. The nearest village is on the plain 600 feet (180 metres) below.

Highlandman's Green at Muthill, 3 miles south of Crieff in Perthshire, was a drovers' stopping place.

Scottish drovers in bonnets and trews with their animals on the journey through Northumberland.

According to Professor E. G. Bowen, a Welsh historian who made an extensive study of droving, Welsh drovers wore the traditional farm labourer's smock, which even in high summer would probably have been perpetually sodden at the hem. So to protect their trousers from the wet they covered them with knee-length woollen stockings, knitted during the long winter evenings by both men and women. These stockings in their turn were protected by leggings, which in the nineteenth century were made of good stout Bristol brown paper, partly waterproofed by being rubbed with soap. Soap was also used on the soles of the stockings, so that when the foot sweated it could slide along the wool instead of blistering by rubbing against the wooden soles of the clogs. The Welsh drover's dress was completed by a wide-brimmed hat. The dapper Smithfield drover depicted in W. H. Pyne's *The Costume of Great Britain* (1805) would never have crossed the mountains of Wales or Scotland in those fancy breeches.

Like all other trades and crafts, the drovers developed their own folklore and superstitions and sang their own work songs and ballads as they rode or tramped with the cattle across the hills. Rowan was considered to be the plant that above all others brought good luck, warding off supernatural evil and natural accidents. Having strictly observed the sabbath, more because the penalties for walking cattle on a Sunday were so

A Smithfield drover, from W. H. Pyne's 'The Costume of Great Britain' (1805). He wears breeches buttoned at the knee over striped stockings, neat shoes and short spats. His drover's licence is fastened to his left arm.

Drovers wore sprigs of rowan for luck and to ward off accidents.

Cilycwm, a Carmarthenshire village which would have been familiar to Dafydd Jones, who likened the souls coming into heaven on judgement day to the cattle converging on the nearby village of Caeo. What appears to be a drain by the cottage doors is actually a drinking trough carefully designed to water the hundreds of cattle passing through the village.

heavy than for any religious conviction, the drovers set off as soon as it was legal to do so, wearing rowan sprigs to ensure a fair journey and good trading. Yet many of them were enthusiastic Christians and more than one Welshman, influenced no doubt by Wesley's preaching tours, made use of his journeys to compose hymns. One we know of was Dafydd Jones of Caeo (north-west of Llandovery), well-known during the eighteenth century at the cattle fairs of Barnet and Maidstone, who used the English he had picked up to translate the hymns of Isaac Watts for his fellow Welshmen.

Considering the dangers drovers had to face, both piety and superstition are easily understandable. As well as the highwaymen and brigands lying in ambush for the drovers, there were also natural perils to be faced, for until the seventeenth century packs of wolves still roamed the wilder moorlands. But probably the drovers' most anxious moments came when water had to be crossed and the lives of both men and beasts were at risk.

In *The Drove Roads of Scotland,* A. R. B. Haldane describes the ferries that brought island cattle to the mainland during the eighteenth and nineteenth centuries. But often there were no boats, and beasts, men and horses had to swim the straits or

On such flat-bottomed boats as these, their decks crowded with Welsh Black cattle, Little Tom of Erwood set out on his last crossing of the Wye. (From W. H. Pyne.)

make a hurried journey across sands at low water. That could be very treacherous indeed. Haldane describes the route from Benbecula to North Uist, across the North Ford, with its 'quicksands ready to trap men or beasts straying from the winding track. Any delay or miscalculation might mean that the inflowing tide would catch a drove in the crossing, when men and cattle would have to swim for their lives. The crossing was thus a hazardous adventure, the recollection of which lives vivid in the memories of those still [1948] alive who shared in it during the last days of the droving industry.'

Other crossings were even more dramatic, like that across the Menai Straits before Telford's bridge joined Anglesey to the mainland. River crossings, too, could be perilous in wet summers when the waters ran high and there is a sad story of the death of a ferryman, affectionately known as Little Tom of Erwood, who for years during the nineteenth century operated the flat-bottomed boat which took cattle across the Wye from the high plateau of Breconshire to the Radnorshire hills. This account comes from an article by Mr E. Jones of Crickhowell, published in the *Western Mail* of 2nd March 1935. He wrote that Little Tom 'was taking a boat load of cattle over when the Wye was in flood, and the cattle in spite of the efforts of the two drovers in charge of them rushed to the side of the boat in terror of the down-coming tide and swamped the boat. The

Grazing in the rich pastures of the Vale of Aylesbury, where cattle from both Scotland and Wales were fattened before their final journey to Smithfield.

drovers saved themselves by clutching at the tails of the animals, and were towed ashore, but Little Tom and his son in their efforts to save the boat were drowned.'

Being used to hazards such as that, it is hardly surprising that, when the toll roads were built, the drovers were prepared to make detours to avoid them, even if they had to go through rough ground and up and down steep inclines to do so. One of the best examples of such an escape route has been traced from the village of Great Witcombe, some 5 miles east of Gloucester. The cattle which were driven along here were Welsh Blacks on their way to the fattening pastures of the Vale of Aylesbury. To avoid the toll gate, these beasts were driven along the green lane to the north of the village and over Birdlip Hill, where they had to make a perilously steep descent back to the main road. The tollgate was put up to pay for the upkeep of road on a one in six gradient, so the severity of the alternative the drovers were prepared to face can be imagined.

Even now mountain cattle can be seen grazing high above the tree line on hill farms, and some of the routes the drovers were prepared to take their beasts along were equally bleak. But they did not travel quickly. An average of 2 miles an hour – the rate that a fell walker generally allows in planning to traverse rough country – was the speed they aimed at; but they usually kept it up for some twelve hours a day. The pace was never forced because the drovers' chief skill was to bring the beasts to their destination in such good condition that after two or three weeks grazing in the English pastures they would be fit enough for market.

The regular pace of the journey must also have been a consideration for the many people who travelled with the drovers in order to have companionship and some measure of safety on their journeys. We know of one woman, Jane Evans of Pumsaint in Carmarthenshire, who went with the drovers in order to enlist as a nurse with Florence Nightingale and sail to the Crimea. Other motives were less altruistic. From the sixteenth century the sons of rich landowners went to London with the drovers to see the world; other lads from more modest backgrounds were sent by their fathers to take up

WHITNEY TOLL BRIDGE ACT, 1797,
36, GEORGE III,
CAP. 56, (VI)
TOLLS,

FOR EVERY HORSE, MARE, GELDING, OX, OR OTHER BEAST DRAWING ANY CARRIAGE THE SUM OF FOURPENCE HALFPENNY,   4½d.

FOR EVERY HORSE, MARE, OR GELDING LADEN OR UNLADEN AND NOT DRAWING THE SUM OF TWOPENCE,   2d.

FOR EVERY PERSON OR FOOT PASSENGER THE SUM OF ONE PENNY,   Id.

FOR EVERY SCORE OF OXEN, COWS, OR NEAT CATTLE THE SUM OF TENPENCE.   10d. AND SO IN PROPORTION FOR ANY GREATER OR LESS NUMBER.

FOR EVERY SCORE OF CALVES, HOGS, SHEEP OR LAMBS, THE SUM OF FIVPENCE,   5d. AND SO IN PROPORTION FOR ANY GREATER OR LESS NUMBER.

A toll-bridge sign at Whitney, Herefordshire. It was here, as they crossed the border into England, that many of the Ceredigion drovers paid their first toll, having cleverly avoided all tolls in Wales by taking mountain routes.

Christopher and John Alcock, two drovers of Barrow, Suffolk. At the end of the nineteenth century they went regularly to Ireland to buy cattle for sale in the Bury St Edmunds market. The overcoats in which they were photographed were given to them by their employers, Freeman Munnings and Thomas Gent of Newmarket.

apprenticeships in the English cities or to read law at the inns of court. Sailors (some of whom were surely jumping ship) used the droves to put a good distance between themselves and the coast, and they in return were used by the drovers to ward off highwaymen and bandits.

These travellers were so much a part of the life of their times, as were the drovers themselves, that we have records of only a

Some of the countryside the Welsh drovers took their cattle across. This high moorland route by the rocks of Pen Cwm above the river Edw was one of the favourite haunts of the Reverend Francis Kilvert, who lived at nearby Clyro. In his diary he mentions encounters with the drovers and tells of searching for the remains of the drovers' inn, which even in his time (the 1860s) had long been out of use.

very few individuals, although it is possible to trace some of the licences granted to drovers in the eighteenth and nineteenth centuries and so discover the basic facts of their existence, their names and places of origin. A few drovers did keep extensive records of their trading and from these it has been possible to reconstruct something of their business life, the way they budgeted for their enterprises and the sort of profits they hoped to make. Sometimes it has even been possible to trace bits of family history. One dealer/drover, David Jonathan of Cardigan, left extensive records of his transactions in the cattle trade during the mid nineteenth century. His account books and those of other members of his family have been meticulously analysed by the agricultural historian Richard Moore-Colyer and quoted in his *Welsh Cattle Drovers*. One of Jonathan's descendants was to become chairman of the Milk Marketing Board; this reminds us of the link between the drovers of the early nineteenth century and the London milkmen, many of whom are Welsh to this day. The connection came about because the drovers often brought milk cows along with the herds of bullocks and made a little money on the side by selling the milk in the few towns they passed through.

Yet much of our knowledge of the drovers is drawn from literature. Rob Roy, immortalised in Sir Walter Scott's novel of that name, has been mentioned. In contrast there is the earthy, plodding Bos of Anglesey, who so infuriated George Borrow by taking him for a fellow drover, for Bos could not 'conceive how any person, either gentle or simple, could have any business in Anglesey save that business was pigs or cattle.'

Bos, as even the indignant Borrow conceded in his *Wild Wales* (1857), was a skilled and educated man (he had been to school in Beaumaris) and so were most of his fellow drovers. It is sad that apart from their names so little is known of these gentlemen of the road. For their knowledge of men, beasts and the countryside of their time must have been immense. But it is not surprising we know so little, for no one bothers to record the ordinary and the drovers with their noisy, stinking herds, which travelled through the villages and delayed men on their shorter daily journeys, must have been an unpopular but common sight in the eighteenth century.

The beasts

CATTLE

Most of the cattle the drovers brought into England from the highlands of both Scotland and Wales were little black animals, often referred to as runts, an expression which related solely to their size and was no reflection on their general hardiness. The Welsh Black, which is an increasingly popular breed in the early twenty-first century, was and still is particularly noted for its ability to thrive on meagre fare (there was an old joke that they did well on the rope used to bind the bales of winter feed for other cattle) and for the way it will put on flesh after a very short spell of good valley grazing (an important consideration for the drovers, who relied on being able to get the animals fit for market in as short a time as possible after the long journey was over).

Welsh Black cattle (upper and lower left) were the breed most usually brought by the drovers from Wales into England, and similar animals came from Scotland. They can thrive on poor feeding and put on flesh quickly when grazing richer lowland pastures; the bullocks were also used as excellent draught animals. The popularity of the breed is again increasing.

Belted Galloways at Boxmoor in Hertfordshire. Polled cattle from Galloway were popular at the Norfolk markets.

The hardiness of drove beasts was put to another purpose. When docile Glamorgan cattle of four or five years growth passed through southern England, their strength and agility made it obvious that they could become good draught oxen and they were so used on the Sussex downs, while the heavier Sussex red cattle worked the land of the farms in the lowlands.

During the eighteenth century the lowlands of Scotland played a leading part in putting into practice the new agricultural techniques that were to revolutionise farming in Britain. One of the most successful of the breeding improvements took place in the Galloway hills in south-west Scotland. Impressively large cattle were produced there, and these animals were sold in great numbers at the East Anglian fairs prior to the turnip-feeding season. These cattle were often polled, partly because it is easier to handle beasts without horns, as many large dairy farms still find today, and partly because of an old folk belief that the growth of horns took up some of the vital juices that should go to the building up of flesh.

Although black was the predominant colour of the animals making up a drove, there was some variety. The West Highland cattle, known as Kyloes from the kyles, streams, rivers and even inlets of the sea which they had to swim across, could be white, red or brindled. They were allowed to keep their long curved horns, as were the black cattle from Castlemartin in Pembrokeshire.

Whatever their breed, the cattle had to be shod for their long journey. As cattle have cloven hoofs, the shoe for each hoof had to be made in two parts, and cattle shoes are generally known as

A pair of ox shoes made by J. Hockham, a blacksmith at Flansham, West Sussex, in 1926. The shoes are 2¹/₄ inches (57 mm) long and are in the collection of the Weald and Downland Open Air Museum, Singleton, West Sussex.

cues (*cws* in Welsh). It takes a special skill and enormous strength to shoe an ox. An anonymous local historian from Builth Wells in mid Wales told how it was done in his pamphlet *The Trail of the Black Ox*: 'The work of cueing was done by throwing a rope with a loop which would drop over the beast; when it reached near the ground it would be pulled tight, drawing the beast's legs together causing it to fall. A man and a boy would then start cueing, the man nailing the cues on and the boy handling the nails; after the end of the small nail was screwed off by a little claw hammer, a slight groove would be made in the hoof with a file, and the end of the nail would be beaten into the hoof. A man and a boy could cue between sixty and seventy cattle a day.'

In *Welsh Cattle Drovers* Dr Richard Moore-Colyer quotes some shoeing costs. He discovered that in the nineteenth century, even after the railways had taken over a great deal of the transport of cattle, a herd of 192 beasts was shod at a cost of £9

The tollhouse at Sicklesmere, Suffolk, outside Bury St Edmunds on the Sudbury road, stood on the route along which Scottish cattle were driven from East Anglian grazing lands to Smithfield. Further down the road was a forge where some of the cattle on the way to London would have been shod.

12s, while the thrower got £3 8s for felling sixty-four runts. In the eighteenth century a smith and his thrower could expect to get between 10d and a shilling for each beast shod.

Sometimes the Scots cattle had shoes only on the outer side of each hoof; and nearly all the cattle were shod with cold iron. In other words, the smiths made the cues in advance of need and brought them to the droves at the start of each journey. But one shoeing would not last the whole of the long trip. Local blacksmiths did well to have their forges sited on the drove routes, and these can still often be found close to the remains of the old inns and grazing lands. Sometimes, too, a smith with a portable forge would accompany the droves on part of the route, to replace cast shoes or to deal with any animal which showed signs of becoming lame.

Cattle disease was the greatest risk to the drovers' finances. Although foot and mouth did not appear in Britain until 1839, outbreaks of murrain were virulent and could put an end to all trading. Several times in the seventeenth century the holding of fairs and markets was prohibited because of outbreaks of the disease. In 1632 no Welsh cattle at all were driven into England and in 1746 there was a particularly virulent outbreak in East Anglia which affected both Welsh and Scottish droves for two years.

In years of cattle plague a drover could expect some compensation for his loss, but the money he received was only a fraction of what he set out to make. We know for instance that in 1754, when William Rowland of Maentwrog in North Wales drove eighty-four beasts to the Kent fairs, he must have returned home a disappointed man, for £12 was all he received in compensation for his cattle afflicted by the plague. Some fifty years later the average sale price for a healthy beast was £5 10s; so Rowland must have been reckoning on at least £4 a head for his, and probably considerably more.

K. J. Bonser quotes a letter from a Dumfriesshire drover, Thomas Bell, written on 31st December 1746 from Hoxne in Suffolk: 'This morning when I went among our beasts there were twenty-nine laid dead in one pasture, worth £5 a head, seventeen in another pasture and eight in another.' Bell does not seem to have expected any compensation, for in a previous letter written on Christmas Day to Bryce Blair, Provost of Annan, who possibly arranged the drove, he laments: 'We cannot get money to bear pocket expenses; all manner of sale is over, our beasts drop in numbers every day . . . our conditions are such that several drovers have run from their beasts and left them dying in the leans and high ways and nobody to own them.'

SHEEP

Although the most spectacular part of the droving trade was concerned with cattle, traditionally England's wealth lay in

Sheep being driven through High Wycombe, Buckinghamshire, in 1900.

This inn sign at Gainsborough, Lincolnshire, and the milestone at Thirsk in North Yorkshire recall the traffic in sheep from the north of England to the London markets.

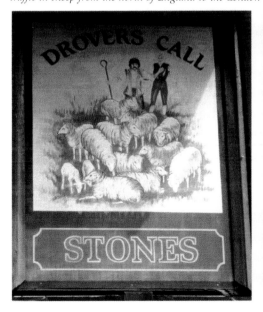

wool, and the movement of sheep from place to place was an important factor in the wool trade. These animals did not travel such long distances, and the driving of sheep still went on after railways had taken over most of the cattle trade. So it is still possible to meet people who have heard first-hand tales of sheep droves. These accounts come mostly from south Wales, England and the Scottish lowlands, for it was considered impossible to take flocks of sheep across wild highland country, where the streams and rivers that could be swum by cattle would present impassable obstacles to sheep.

From the early nineteenth century, droves of sheep began to predominate over cattle and the names of many of the shepherds are known to us. Among them is Bill Thatcher of Gedney, Lincolnshire. In his extreme old age, at the beginning of the twentieth century, he was still taking sheep to London via Norwich. He reckoned to take about a week on the journey and to handle between five and six hundred sheep. Some decades before that, sheep were being taken regularly from Northumberland and the Scottish borders to the newly established hill farms of Exmoor. It was thought by Frederic Knight, who then owned most of those farms, that the hardy Cheviot sheep were well suited to withstanding a moorland winter. So they were driven south overland or taken by ship to Portishead and taken west from there.

PIGS

Pigs were driven for comparatively short distances only and, considering the enormous size that these animals were bred to, it is amazing that they could be moved at all. Yet it was done, the average daily length of a journey being 6 miles. Most pig droving took place from Wales and the West Country, great numbers being driven east out of Cornwall. Bristol was one of the great pig markets but many were driven further east. S. and B. Webb in *The Story of the King's Highway* (Longman's Green, 1913) report that in 1830 14,500 pigs from Ireland passed through the turnpike at Beckhampton, Wiltshire, en route for London. In Wales pigs from the south were mostly driven to Sully, south-west of Cardiff, and shipped across to Bridgwater on the Somerset coast. From there they were either sold direct to local farmers for fattening or taken on to the Bristol markets.

It was probably some of the latter that George Borrow met, being driven along the road to Llangollen. Among them was one that was muzzled (a fairly frequent practice) and which was of remarkable size, weighing about 'eighteen score of pounds'. Not surprisingly, it 'walked with considerable difficulty'. In Borrow's time pigs were changing hands at eighteen to twenty shillings, but the cost was not the only worry for the purchaser. Pigs are among the least tractable of domesticated animals (hence the muzzles) and Borrow

Pigs, despite their size, managed to walk about 6 miles a day, sometimes wearing boots to protect their trotters.

reported that 'dire was the screaming of the porkers, yet the purchaser invariably seemed to know how to manage his bargain, keeping the left arm round the body of the swine and with the right hand fast grasping the ear – some few are led away by strings'.

Anyone who has experienced the obstinacy of pigs will appreciate the skill these men exercised. But pigs were relatively fortunate in the matter of shoeing. According to Professor E. G. Bowen, their trotters were sometimes protected by little woollen boots with leather soles.

GEESE

Geese were moved about all over Britain, but the most notable goose drove was from Lincolnshire and the Fens to the Michaelmas Goose Fair in Nottingham. As the geese were driven there at the end of harvest, they were able to feed on the stubble in the fields along the way.

The phrase 'to shoe a goose' has often been used to stand for an attempt to do the impossible or to spend a lot of time trifling with foolish business. K. J. Bonser instances a misericord of about 1430 in Whalley Abbey in Lancashire, showing a smith standing in his smithy preparing to shoe a goose tethered to a stump of wood. Below it is an inscription which can be roughly transcribed as 'He who meddles with what another does had better go home and shoe his goose'.

Yet the webbed feet of the geese were prepared for droving. The birds were driven through a pan of tar mixed with sawdust, grit and in some places ground oyster shells. This made a sort of pad for the soles of their feet. Bonser also discovered some instances where real pads of felt were attached to the geese.

P. G. Hughes in *Wales and the Drovers* (1943) tells of a Welsh smith who fastened blunt spikes an inch or so long to the pads

of tar, which were sealed into place as the tar hardened. The noise and confusion which accompanied this operation must have been immense.

TURKEYS

In the early years of the eighteenth century Daniel Defoe in his *Tour through England and Wales* recorded that 'at least three hundred droves of turkeys (for they drive them all in droves on foot) pass in one season over Stratford Bridge'. The bridge he was referring to is the one that crosses the Stour on the Ipswich to Colchester road, and the numbers of turkeys to each drove varied between three hundred and a thousand.

Over the years the trade increased, Norfolk turkeys in particular proving an immensely profitable business. There is no evidence that the feet of turkeys were prepared in any way for the journey, and it would probably not have been practical for them to carry any extra weight of any sort, for at night it was usual for the droves to stop at some place where the birds could roost in the trees. This meant that they had to be hand-fed as the corn could not just be scattered on the ground to attract rats and foxes.

DOGS AND HORSES

To help them in their task the drovers were dependent on both dogs and horses. In Scotland the drovers shared their

Blewburton Buzzard 'Ban', a Cardiganshire working corgi that belonged to Dr K. Linacre of Didcot. Note the long tail, large ears and slightly domed head, which distinguish this breed from the more familiar Pembrokeshire corgi. They weigh between 30 and 40 pounds (13–18 kg) and are extremely tough and hardy animals.

*A working corgi 'heeling' a Friesian cow
into the cowshed.*

oatmeal with great brown and white dogs, a breed which is
depicted in Landseer's painting. In Wales the favoured breed
for work with cattle was the corgi, a dog which runs so close to
the ground that it can easily avoid the hoofs of any bullock that
may kick out.

In 1811, in *A Treatise on Breeding Livestock*, R. Parkinson made
a strong claim for the dogs of Dorset, which had long soft hair.
It was claimed that the smaller they were the better they were
able to handle cattle. Most cattle drovers relied on the black and
white collies, which are still the most popular farm dogs, used
especially for working sheep. The drovers' cattle dogs, which
were often somewhat larger, were given the name 'coally', a
term which could also be applied to a black-faced sheep.

Both Scots and Welsh dogs were larger and fiercer than those
generally used for sheep. They were of enormous intelligence
and frequently found their own way home from the south-east,
if their masters should want to stay and spend a profitable time
working in the autumn harvests. Haldane relates how, as a
child in the 1840s, Miss Stewart Mackenzie of Brahan in Ross-
shire asked her parents why she came across so many
unaccompanied dogs obviously making their way northwards.
She was told that 'these were dogs belonging to drovers who

The cur was a favourite working dog in the north of England. Thomas Bewick, who made this engraving, described the cur as a 'trusty and useful servant to the farmer and grazier'.

had taken cattle to England and that when the droving was finished the drovers returned by boat to Scotland. To save the trouble and expense of their transport the dogs were turned loose to find their own way north. It was explained that the dogs followed the routes taken on the southward journey, being fed at inns or farms where the drove had "stanced" and that in the following year when the droves were again on the way south they paid for the food given to the dogs'. Mary Russell Mitford, in *Our Village*, gives us a clue as to what these dogs might expect to be given at the inns. Jack Bint's collie dog Watch, employed to drive sheep from Salisbury Plain to Smithfield, was 'accustomed to live chiefly on bread and beer'.

Some of the Welsh drovers in later years made the return journey by coach, and so their dogs too had to find their own way home. We know the name of one of them, Cailo, who came from Llandrillo in Denbighshire. Cailo even had to carry the pony's saddle home for, like many drovers, his master sold his mount along with the cattle at the English fairs. This sale was reckoned as part of the general economics of the droving trade; for although many of the drovers' assistants made the journey on foot, the top men always rode.

The Welsh drovers were mounted on sturdy cobs or on the ancestors of the ponies that still run half-wild on the Welsh hills, themselves descendants of the Arab packhorses brought over by the Romans.

Fairs and markets

Some of the leading drovers were also cattle dealers and owned the beasts they drove. Usually they preferred to buy the bullocks privately from local farmers, but in addition great numbers of cattle also changed hands at the annual fairs of Wales and Scotland. (Auctioneers were not introduced until the latter part of the nineteenth century.)

One of the most important of these was the tryst at Crieff to the west of Perth, where the Michaelmas market in the eighteenth century might handle over thirty thousand cattle. Later the tryst moved south to Falkirk, which lies between Edinburgh and Stirling. Here cattle from the Highlands were sold to the dealers who arranged for their journey to the south. The tryst (a word that comes from 'trust') or fair was held three times a year, in August, September and October. The tryst was always on the second Tuesday of each month, so that nobody would be tempted to drive cattle on the sabbath. Although the droves were a regular part of life for the people living locally, to visitors they were a source of wonder, as Dorothy Wordsworth discovered when she came to describe her encounter with Highland cattle and their drovers on the way to the Falkirk Tryst on 14th September 1803. The cattle bought there in the earlier months were frequently resold at St Faith's fair, held at Horsham St Faith near Norwich during the first part of October. In 1727 Daniel Defoe reported that he was well

The Drovers' Hall at the Metropolitan Cattle Market included facilities for the delivery of lectures 'and other means of improving the minds of this class of our fellow countrymen who need it not a little'.

prepared to believe the estimate that forty thousand Scots cattle were bought by Norfolk graziers each year and that most of the business was done at St Faith's. For, as he wrote, 'These Scots runts as they call them, coming out of the cold and barren mountains of the Highlands in Scotland, feed so eagerly on the rich pastures in these marshes, that they thrive in an unusual manner, and grow monstrously fat; and the beef is so delicious for taste, that the inhabitants prefer 'em to the English cattle'.

The marshes that Defoe referred to are those lying between Norwich, Beccles and Great Yarmouth. Defoe also noted that those cattle that were kept over in East Anglia were fattened on

turnips during the winter months. At one time settlement for all deals made in the area was concluded at the Angel Inn at North Walsham. That inn no longer exists but the block of flats which has replaced it retains its façade and name. The beasts that the Norfolk graziers did not keep for their own consumption were driven the following September to the London markets at Smithfield or to the great Barnet Fair. In 1818 Arthur Young, in a report for the Board of Agriculture, reckoned that the expense of taking cattle the 112 miles from Norfolk to Smithfield would work out at 7s 1$^{1}/_{2}$d per head.

Jim Proudfoot's illustration of the tryst at Crieff is part of the Highland Drovers exhibition (by MKW Design Partnership) at the Crieff Visitor Centre in Perthshire.

The Angel Inn at North Walsham in Norfolk was used as a centre for concluding business between drovers and graziers. No longer an inn, the façade fronts modern flats.

Cattle from North Wales were frequently fattened in the Vale of Aylesbury and then taken on to the market at Banbury. Others were driven further east and fattened on the salt marshes of Essex and Kent. They were then either sold locally at Canterbury, Maidstone or Chilham or driven back west to Smithfield. Those cattle from South Wales that had changed hands at Bristol market were often bound for St Catherine's Fair near Guildford, where they changed hands again before the journey to Smithfield.

The archives relating to these fairs are one source of our knowledge about the drovers. From medieval times we have

St Catherine's Hill, south of Guildford, Surrey, was the site of an important market and fair, painted by J. M. W. Turner. Drovers brought Welsh cattle from Bristol here to sell on to Smithfield.

documents relating to the charters under which the fairs were established and the laws by which they were regulated. Later records sometimes give an indication of the prices that were realised for the beasts. Sheep were also included in the great markets. By 1812 it was reckoned that some twenty-five thousand sheep appeared annually at the Falkirk Tryst.

The slaughterman, from Pyne's 'The Costume of Great Britain', signified the end of the drove.

The drovers' routes

It is not possible to give a complete gazetteer of all the drove routes of Britain; the following list simply gives a few examples from the hundreds of roads and trackways throughout the country which were regularly used by the drovers and which can still be traced today. Many of them are in wild and beautiful country and make good drives or walks – examples of which are described in the next chapter.

SCOTLAND

Argyll. From the island of Mull the cattle were ferried to Oban, and from Islay and Jura they either took the short and often dangerous crossing to Craignish in the north, or the longer, safer way south to Loch Tarbert in Knapdale. Some of these animals were intended for the markets at Dumbarton, but from 1770 onwards most of them were driven to the trysts at Falkirk. The various ways they went have been described in detail in A. R. B. Haldane's *The Drovers' Roads of Scotland,* but visitors today will find that the most interesting routes to follow lie to the west. The northern road from Oban went to Tyndrum via Taynuilt, the Pass of Brander, Dalmally and Glen Lochy.

The Portway across Long Mynd, near Church Stretton in Shropshire, is now a long-distance footpath but was once an important drove route.

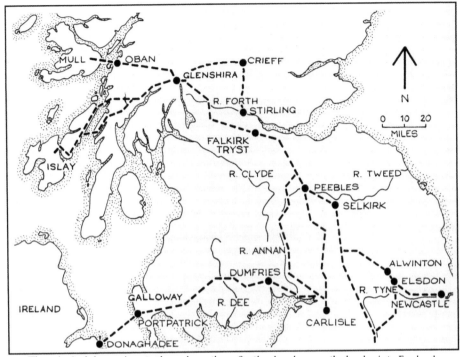

The principal drovers' route through southern Scotland and across the border into England.

From Craignish many of the beasts went to the market at Kilmichael Glassary before being taken from Loch Awe-side to Inveraray. From there they went east to Falkirk by way of Ardlui at the head of Loch Lomond.

Southern Scotland. The cattle from the Falkirk Tryst mostly entered England at Carlisle, where they were joined by those which had been brought across from Ireland to Portpatrick and by the herds from Galloway. Again the routes are described in detail by Haldane. He is convinced that a few droves went to the south-east at the beginning of their journey, crossing the Pentland Hills to Peebles over the pass known as the Cauldstane Slap.

The Drovers' Inn at East Linton is close to the Great North Road, the A1 from Edinburgh to Newcastle. The bagpipes may be artistic licence.

NORTH OF ENGLAND

Maiden Way. Many Scots cattle were driven along the course of this Roman road, which runs from the Bewcastle Fells in Northumberland over Hadrian's Wall and goes on to Kirkby Thore near Appleby in Cumbria. Between Alston and Kirkland it runs over Melmerby Fell and through Gilderdale Forest. The northern part of the road is the one which Sir Walter Scott imagined his two drovers taking on their last and tragic drove.

The Hambleton Drove. The best-known of the northern droveways follows the prehistoric route over the Hambleton Hills between Durham and York. You can walk along a 15 mile stretch of this way, starting from Swainby, just off the A172 at the northern edge of Osmotherley Moor, and following the drove south along the Hambleton Hills to Sutton Bank south of Scotch Corner and east of Thirsk.

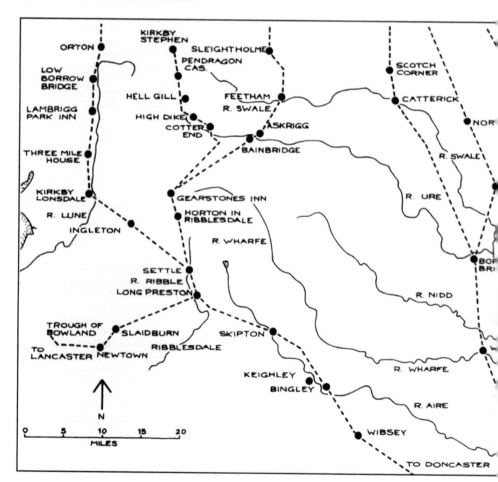

Part of the Hambleton Drove, between Durham and York, can now be followed by walkers on the Cleveland Way. This is the way at Hesketh Dyke, north of Sutton Bank.

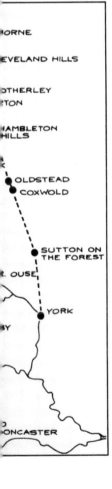

IORNE

EVELAND HILLS

OTHERLEY
TON

HAMBLETON
HILLS

● OLDSTEAD
● COXWOLD

● SUTTON ON
THE FOREST

R. OUSE

● YORK

BY

D
ONCASTER

The principal drovers' routes through the Pennines and Yorkshire.

EAST ANGLIA

The Harling Drove. Unlike most of the ancient roads and tracks in the northern part of East Anglia, which run from north to south, the droves go from west to east. The one which at its eastern end is known as the Harling Drove does, however, go south, following a track of great antiquity. You can follow it by lanes and forest paths from Hockwold-cum-Wilton in the Fens, through Weeting to the west of Grimes Graves, through Thetford Forest, along the lane to the north of Croxton, across Croxton Heath and East Wretham nature reserve to Roundham Heath, where the drove joins the Peddar's Way just north of the A11.

The Icknield Way, which runs through East Anglia to the Oxfordshire and Berkshire Ridgeway, is rightly associated with the ancient British tribe of the Iceni. However, K. J Bonsor points out that the name also derives from *iken*, the old word for ox, thus signifying the route as a long-established drove.

The church of St Andrew at Roudham in Norfolk was ruined in the 1730s but has remained a landmark on the drove road from the fenland of the Great Ouse to East Harling.

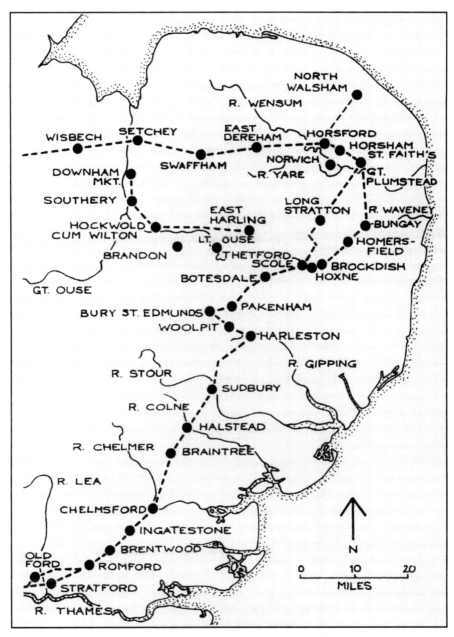

The principal drovers' routes in East Anglia.

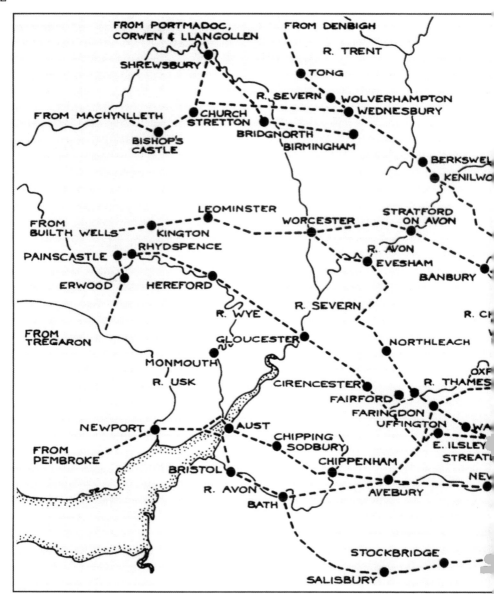

WALES

The most famous and dramatic of the Welsh drove routes runs across the high, wild land, generally known as the Welsh desert, which stretches to the east of the river Teifi. A mountain road covers the drove linking Tregaron (to the south of Aberystwyth) with Abergwesyn (to the west of Builth Wells). It makes an exciting 14 mile stretch.

The principal drovers' routes from Wales to the London area.

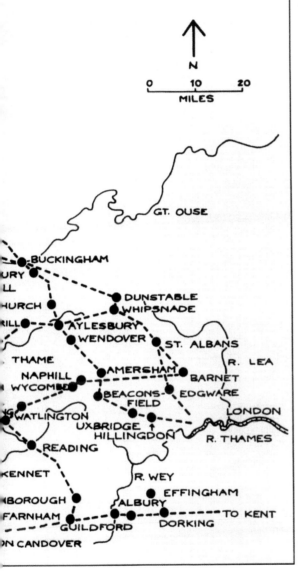

Some of the cattle from the market at Tregaron were fattened on the rich pastures along the banks of the Tywi as it flows through Carmarthen and Llandeilo. On their way to England they converged at Pumsaint to the east of Lampeter, and it is possible to follow some of their ways on foot or horseback through the hills bordering the Cothi valley to the north-west of Llandovery. It was there in the sixteenth century that Twm Sion

Cattle on the sands near the estuary at Porthmadog, from which many Welsh cattle started their journey east.

Catti, the drover outlaw of folklore and an historical mayor of Brecon, performed his legendary feats.

THE SOUTH OF ENGLAND

Many of the drovers from South Wales brought heavy knitting to sell in the Farnham stocking fair on their way to the Kent markets. They converged at Stockbridge, and part of their way eastwards can now be followed by taking the footpath that runs due east from the lane between Stoke Charity and Kings Worthy and which comes out on the A33 opposite the Lunway Inn. The journey continues east along lanes and footpaths to the south of Preston Candover.

From the Guildford markets, the way east went either by the ridgeway track now designated as the long-distance walk of the North Downs Way or along the ancient Pilgrims' Way to Canterbury.

FINDING DROVE ROADS

All the main drove roads were crossed by green lanes used for driving cattle short distances to local markets. No one has undertaken the task of mapping the whole network of droveways in Britain, and it would probably be impossible to do so. To trace them for yourself look out for the following signs:

1. Place names: Welsh Ways and other such names for roads or lanes in the English countryside; the word drove or drift used to designate a lane; Halfpenny Lanes and Halfpenny Fields; inns called 'The Drovers' or 'The Black Ox' all indicate that Welsh or Scottish droves once passed that way.

Indications of drove ways are names such as Halfpenny Lane (this one is at Cholsey, Oxfordshire, above), inns like the Black Bull (this one at Thirsk in North Yorkshire, below) and wide verges, as on this drove road on the Long Mountain by Welshpool (right).

2. Lanes running between banks that are often well to the side of the present track or footpath, indicating wide grazing verges on each side of it. Often you will find traces of hawthorn on these banks, the relics of ancient hedges marking the course of the drove.

3. Outstanding trees: in Wales the quick-growing Scots pines were often planted on open hillsides to indicate the drove routes and to show where the drovers' inns were situated. On the chalklands of southern England yew served the same purpose. In some places more exotic trees were used. In the scrub and beechwoods of Naphill Common near High

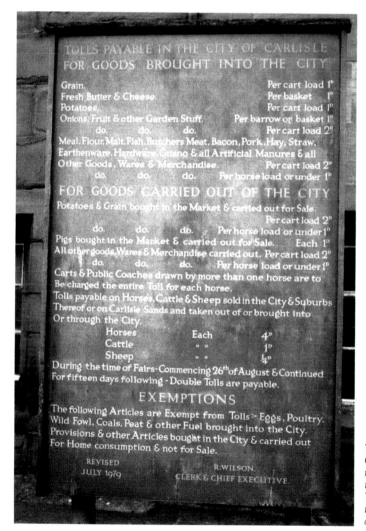

The toll board for Carlisle. The city did not exempt drovers as recommended by Thomas Telford and indeed charged them double during fairs.

Wycombe in Buckinghamshire a Portuguese laurel indicates where the drovers once found overnight shelter.

Locating the drovers' inns is one good way of establishing routes, for, as the Anglesey drover, Bos, boasted to George Borrow, 'there is not a public house between here and Worcester at which I am not known'. Many other drovers could, no doubt, have made similar claims.

From the beginning of the nineteenth century, the drovers' routes over much of the common land of England were affected by the Enclosure Acts, which forced the cattle on to the main thoroughfares. Indeed, in the early 1800s De Quincey commented on the 'vast droves of cattle upon the Great North Road', now the A1.

The drovers were also affected by the introduction of tolls, although the bridge-builder and highway engineer Thomas Telford advised authorities in Perthshire and Stirlingshire that the tolls should be relaxed for cattle at the time of the markets. His argument was that the time that would be taken by the drovers in making the payments would hold up all other traffic. In a few places his case prevailed. However, such concessions were a rare exception and frequently the drovers chose to make difficult and even hazardous diversions in order to avoid toll payment. Richard Moore-Colyer has pointed out, however, that this was not always the wisest choice, for the time lost in negotiating the diversions often proved more costly than the toll charges.

Walking drove roads

Wales: the Old Harlech Road (OS Landranger 124)

Pont Scethin (634235) is the old bridge that once carried coach traffic between London and Harlech. It is also part of the drove road from North Wales going east towards Dolgellau. To reach the bridge, take the lane to the north of Talybont (588224) leading east and then follow the footpath east towards the mountain ridge of the Rhinogs. If you want to walk some of the droveway from Pont Scethin, you must climb south over the hills towards the lane at 657202, which will take you to Bontddu and the A496 going east to Dolgellau.

Wales: west from Machynlleth (OS Landranger 135)

The cattle going east from Machynlleth (745009) would have followed the valley of the Dovey, a route now taken by the railway and the A489. At the junction of Cemmaes Road on the A489 (823045) the drove ran east towards Newtown. This way goes through some very dramatic scenery, and there are several footpaths that you might like to take, overlooking the droveway. One is reached from the lane that goes south-east from Abergwydol (792029) and then runs north-east over Comins Bach to Cemmaes Road. That way does involve a stiff climb. A gentler walk lies north of the railway from Pont Doldwymyn (826046) and runs east to Commins Uchaf (846035), where a lane takes you back to the main road.

A drovers' road across the Berwyn mountains.

Wales: the Berwyns (OS Landranger 125)

The A5 runs west from Llangollen, south of which are the Berwyn mountains. There is a spectacular walk across them, between Corwen (078433), one of the most important meeting points for the drovers of North Wales, and Llanarmon Dyffryn Ceiriog (158328). It is best to start by walking through Coed y Glyn (043386), between Llandrillo and Cynwyd on the B4401 to the south of Corwen. From there you will reach the open hills and the track going east-south-east past the memorial stone at 091367. From there the track goes east through Nant Rhydwilym to join the road on the west bank of the Ceiriog river to Llanarmon Dyffryn Ceiriog, a distance of some 13 miles.

Walking the drovers' way along the Kerry Ridgeway (above) and the former drovers' inn at Anchor (below).

Wales/Shropshire: the Kerry Ridgeway (OS Landranger 136)
    East of Newtown, this long-distance footpath is now signed
from Cider House Farm, once a drovers' inn (108845). It heads
north-east along the ridge above Kerry, going past two tumuli
and over the B4368, through a conifer forest and then over two
fields to Kerry Pole, a weathervane with a fox on top of it. A
mile or so downhill to the south brings you over the Shropshire
border to the village of Anchor and the B4368. The inn at
Anchor was a well-known drovers' hostelry, much used by
those who had driven the herds along this ridge to avoid
paying tolls.

Wales: Black Mountains (OS Landranger 161)
    The section of Offa's Dyke Path that runs east of Capel-y-ffin
(254314) will take you above the lane to the west going over
Gospel Pass (236352) into Hay-on-Wye, along which cattle from
Brecon would have been brought into England. You can either
follow the Dyke Path to the Wye by Hay Bridge, or take one of
the footpaths going steeply downhill to join the lane north of
Gospel Pass at 240367.

Yorkshire: the Hambleton Drove (OS Landranger 93, 99 and 100)
    A stretch of this important drove route from Scotland
towards the Vale of York runs across Whorlton Moor at the

The Hambleton Inn, where the Wordsworths saw a drove of Scottish cattle.

The Icknield Way near West Wratting in Cambridgeshire.

northern edge of the Cleveland Hills, starting by Swainby, just off the A172 (478020). Follow the road going south to Osmotherley. After about a mile leave the road by the footbridge at Sheepwash. Cross the stream here to the north of a plantation and you will come to High Lane Track, a part of the Hambleton Drove running south to the Chequers Inn, on the road to Hawnby. The Chequers, once a drovers' inn, is now a farm shop and tea room. If you want to follow the drove further to the south, head out across the hills, on the Cleveland Way, a long-distance footpath, going south along a track past Limekiln House (the remains of another drovers' inn) for some 14 miles until you reach the Hambleton Inn on the A170 (522829). It was here that Dorothy Wordsworth noted in her diary that she and William saw a drove of 'little Scotch cattle' who 'panted and tossed fretfully about'.

East Anglia: the Icknield Way (OS Landranger 154)
    Much of the Icknield Way connecting East Anglia to London

The Harling Drove crosses the nature reserve at East Wretham, Norfolk, on its way to East Harling.

Ferry Lane at Moulsford, Oxfordshire, where the droveway reached the river Thames.

now lies under the M11. However, there are stretches that run parallel to it along which the droves were taken. One such goes from Green End Farm (north-west of West Wratting, 594532) and then runs directly south-west past West Watting Grange to the Black Bull Inn (579508) on the B1052 to the west of Balsham.

East Anglia: the Harling Drove (OS Landranger 144)

This is an ancient drove route connected with the many drovers' ways leading from St Faith's Fair near Norwich and going south-west towards Brandon and Thetford, where much of the area is now under military control. However, it is possible to follow the route of the drove by the lane going west from the southern bank of Fowl Mere (878894) through the forest to the A134. From there the drove becomes a track going west through the forest to the A1065, south-east of Weeting.

The Oxfordshire and Berkshire Ridgeway (OS Landranger 174)

A good 'two car walk' (i.e. one at each end) runs east between East Ilsley, the site of a great sheep fair (494813), and Halfpenny Lane, leading down, beside an old drovers' grazing ground, to Cholsey and Moulsford. From East Ilsley take the marked Ridgeway path along the top of the downs. It goes north-east for about 2 miles and then turns abruptly to the south-east. The droveway, however, continues north-east along the Fair Mile to Cholsey Downs, before dropping steeply to meet the main A417 road at 574838 between Blewbury and Streatley.

The way to Hereford (OS Landranger 148)
   North of the Wye and south of the Roman road covered by the A438, a droveway runs from The Scar (354445) 2 miles to Monnington on Wye. You can leave it by the lane, joining the A438 to Hereford, at Portway. However, it is also possible to follow the drove a further 2 miles east to Byford (395426) and join the A438 about a mile to the west of Bridge Sollers (415425). This drove would have dodged the Portway toll into Hereford.

Gloucestershire: Birdlip Hill (OS Landranger 162 and 163)
   To avoid the tolls around Gloucester, the drovers took cattle up the steep slope of Birdlip Hill, which now joins the southern end of the Cotswold Way long-distance footpath. To get some idea of their climb, follow that section of the Cotswold Way which runs north-west of Cirencester. This means leaving the A46 between Stroud and Cheltenham just by the minor road going east to High Brotheridge (894137). To the east of this junction, the Cotswold Way climbs steeply through Witcombe Wood to the west of Birdlip (925145), a distance of 3 miles. From here the Roman road of Ermin Street (now the A417) goes south-east to Cirencester.

Hampshire: Stockbridge to Preston Candover (OS Landranger 185)
   From the old drovers' inn at Stockbridge (360350) you can follow the drovers' way north-east to Preston Candover by taking the A30 and then heading east from Sutton Scotney on minor roads to Micheldever and on to the A33. Follow the A33 south for 2 to 3 miles to the Lunway Inn and a minor road leading to the B3046 at Northington for Preston Candover. To walk part of the drove route to the west of the Lunway (itself a major drove route), turn south at Stoke Charity (488394) and take the minor road as far as 483363. Here a footpath heading east takes you along the drove, under a railway line and back to the Lunway Inn.

Essex: Epping Forest (OS Landranger 166 and 167)
   The nearest grazing rounds to London's Smithfield market that you can visit now lie in Epping Forest. There was once a cattle market as well as grazing land for the drovers on Wanstead Flats, between Leytonstone and Wanstead, and another on Epping Plain (468033), north of Epping, where the Bell Inn was once a drovers' hostelry. A remaining stretch of the drove road called Clapgate Lane runs south-west towards Waltham Abbey from Aimes Green (397028), south of Nazeing. Puck Lane, another droveway, runs from Aimes Green west towards Fisher's Green.

Further reading

Addison, William. *English Fairs and Markets*. Batsford, 1953.

Bonsor, K. J. *The Drovers*. Macmillan, 1970.

Godwin, Fay, and Toulson, Shirley. *The Drovers' Roads of Wales*. Wildwood House, 1977.

Haldane, A. R. B. *The Drovers' Roads of Scotland*. Edinburgh, 1952.

Hughes, Philip Gwyn. *Wales and the Drovers*. Golden Grove Book Company, 1988. (Originally published in 1943.)

Moore-Colyer, Richard. *Roads and Trackways of Wales*. Landmark, 2000.

Moore-Colyer, Richard. *Welsh Cattle Drovers*. Landmark, 2002.

Saunders, Roy. *The Drovers' Highway*. Oldbourne, 1959.

Toulson, Shirley, and Forbes, Caroline. *The Drovers' Roads of Wales: Pembrokeshire and the South*. Whittet Books, 1992.

Sheepwash Pond on The Ridgeway at Mill Hill in north London was used by drovers as they neared their journey's end.

The drove road by Muggleswick Smithy, west of Consett, County Durham, was used by Scottish drovers on their journey south.

Places to visit

The Heritage Centre, Kings Road, Town Centre, Llandovery, Carmarthenshire SA20 0AW. Telephone: 01550 720693. Website: www.breconbeacons.org

The Highland Drovers Exhibition, Crieff Visitor Centre, Muthill Road, Crieff, Perthshire PH7 4HQ. Telephone: 01764 654014. Website: www.crieff.co.uk

Former drove routes offer walkers clear paths across some of Britain's finest countryside, like this stretch of the Oxfordshire Ridgeway.

Index